I0173239

Shades Of My Soul

Reflections of what's Within

RASHEEN DOUGLAS

/ BookLeaf
Publishing
India | USA | UK

Made with ❤ on the BookLeaf Publishing Platform
www.bookleafpub.in
www.bookleafpub.com

Dedication

This is dedicated to a lady that I always will love. One that sparked me to become a better me. I will always love you. I continue to pray for you daily for you to gain true healing from this journey called life. I always will believe in you to be able to do so. I'll see you in one day in the 5D.

I will always love you Natasha

Preface

This book is inspired by the different trials and tribulations I've experienced in my life. Life is about moments. I share a few of them in this book

Acknowledgements

I like to thank my family, friends, and close relationships with people I loved. I like to thank Bookleaf Publishing for this challenge they had as well. I like to thank a person I will always cherish and love. Lastly, I would like thank the Divine for loving me and allowing me to share pieces of my heart

1. I've Always Seen You

I've always seen you
The world has never been kind to you
It always seems despite how much the sun shined you
remain in the dark
It seems no one cared about your heart
All these years hiding brokenness I still see you
Though at times you might want to give up
Know that I'm still beside you rooting for you
Those nights you've been alone I saw the tears
when no one was around to console your pain
I also felt your pain deep within
Know when your tears fell I cried myself
I've always seen you
I see the manufactured smile you wear for the crowd
Not wanting to reveal the hard days you held within
Desiring to release what's bottled deep within
Yet you pause scared to be judged so you continue to die
inside
So you remain quiet fearing that no one will accept you
Know that I always accept and treasure you

For you're so special and your heart is so giving
No one sees how much love you have for others
It's gets lost because you're not able to display that side
of you
Know that you're always loved because I've always seen
you

2. Middle Man

I apologize
For the times he wasn't soft enough
I apologize
For the times he didn't open up
He never had a place before you that he felt it was okay
He had to learn after you that it wasn't the best way
I apologize
For the times there were moments he made you feel
unheard
I think he struggled himself from him having his voice
that had been deferred
I apologize
If any of his actions made you feel that you weren't
enough
Just know he saw something in you to say for him you
were always enough
Just know he saw himself always inside of you
He always admired the strength that resided in you
I apologize
If he ignited any insecurities you already had

Please know he feels he lost out on greatest treasure God
let him have
I apologize
If his absence has made you feel that he didn't care
It's quite the opposite he left to show how much he dared
I apologize
For the times he put pressure on you to feel validation
He's learned that self love is the best way to combat that
is his revelation
I apologize
That things ended like it did
But know being away from you tore him up within
Know that there's not a day that you don't cross his mind
But I think you already know this deep inside
I believe he wishes there was another chapter in
you two's story
No matter what happens I'm apologizing to let you know
his side of the story

3. Love is Needed

This world needs so much healing
It breaks my heart to see
It's like the world right now is truly the Devil's
playground
No matter where you go there's so much hate
It's like the main dish being served on everyone's plate
There's so much division that's taking place
Through politics, race, and even gender
This has always been the plan but people have been slow
to conceive it
The elites and their Satanic regime have always planned
this up their sleeve
This has been their plan that has been many years in the
making
Little do they know there is a movement that is
happening with God's chosen people
It's been a mission to raise this planet's vibration so they
will ultimately lose
Whether you refer to the Creator as Source, God, or even
Divine it's totally fine

The movement really is to treat everyone with the
emotion of love
We've been so programmed to accept this system that
we've been given
People don't realize the world we have grown into has
been a system to keep our vibrations suppressed
They purposely created the system to keep us operating
in fear
From working these jobs to stress out to not being able
to raise kids our adequately
Doing so they've kept our people developing trauma
That trauma gets passed down every generation making
us worse and not ready for tomorrow
That time is over for along with myself with a group of
people being generational curse breakers
These group people are here to awaken the masses to a
new world we should live in
One that is unified by the divinity that resides in all
We all should share in movement to genuinely interact
with each other in the name of love

4. Man with Sensitivity

I've learned to love me
I know that I'm not everyone's cup of tea
I've learned to love me
I used to question why I was cursed with sensitivity
I've learned to love me
There were times I thought I lost out on women I wanted
to date for this quality
I've learned to love me
At times being a man I hated this part of me
I've learned to love me
There were times in my relationships I was told I had too
much emotion
I've learned to love me
I used to turn my sensitivity down to be accepted I guess
as a form of protection
I've learned to love me
This supposed curse I now cherish as a gift
I've learned to love me
I recognize that this gift helps me treat people with
empathy

I learned to love me
Having this gift has allowed me to move with more
compassion during my interactions
I learned to love me
This has allowed me to practice a greater sense of
discernment and intuition
I've learned to love me
I now truly appreciate the way I was built because I can
have the greatest connections
For those who have issues accepting all of me I know
now they don't truly love me

5. Emotional Intelligence

I'm learning to not check the person
It's all about the behavior
You have to realize there's always an underlying reason
I'm not saying to accept the unwelcomed behavior
I'm simply saying don't judge them for it
You don't always know the person's back story
Have some grace for people with some understanding
I'm grateful to become in knowledge of this
For I'm no better than the next person
There's plenty of times I've known I've been guilty of
hurting another
If the Divine can love us and accept us for all we've done
I'm not bigger than the Divine
So how can little ol me not forgive others cuz when God
can forgive all of us
I have nothing to gain by keeping grudges
It won't affect the other person if I don't, it will just leave
me broken
It's just a waste of good energy
Whether it's a friend or an enemy, I just wish them the

best

Just to the enemy they just can do it somewhere else For

I just move out of love, I won't have to lift a hand

If I live for the Divine my battles are already won

6. Wishing I Knew

Daily I ask the Divine to work on me
I know the collapse of my union was ultimately on me
Maybe at one point I prayed for wisdom so I may be able
to see
I guess I forgot what I asked for but now info flows to
me like the tides in the sea
I heard the coldest line earlier today to spark self
reflection
The line was being the frame makes it hard to see the
picture
Hearing that was definitely something I could relate to
I've already been in hermit mode just soaking up
knowledge like as a sponge
Just that line was so cold it spoke to my soul
I'm constantly praying to the Divine for me to truly
forgive myself
I battle almost everyday to not beat myself up for
shattering such a beautiful gift
Daily while learning when I look back I find more and
more mistakes

From not praying for us to not accurately labeling my
bad habits caused by my internal trauma state
I can look back and actually see where I allowed outside
influence break an already rocky foundation
At the end of the day I know as the man in this
partnership I allowed this situation
Now facing divorce it's rough learning all I know
Wishing I sought this knowledge before the
commitment
Yet I know on the other hand I know there was a reason
the Divine allowed it
Everything that happens in the universe isn't happening
by chance
All I can do now is continue to learn in case I'm
fortunate enough to have another heart in my hands

7. Trusting God's Process

They say things get easier with time
I'm just waiting for time to align with me to feel that
inside
I just try to pray to God for strength during this time
So many times I've wanted to write to let you know were
on my mind
It's so hard knowing I don't have you anymore
Even more so now that I truly know you're the lady that
is supposed to be with me
I pray one day soon you'll see what I see
There was nothing like you in my life
I just need you to know what real life should look like
I just needed to leave to break what we were going
through
It was a terrible cycle that wasn't going to change
I knew nothing was going to change by staying with you
Real change happens when real loss happens
I didn't leave to jump into another relationship
I have no desire to have anyone else in my space
No one can replace you in this life queen

I need you to always be my co-star in every scene
I just want you to reciprocate the same love I present to
you
You wasn't going to gain clarity by experience or doing
the work
I was praying you would gain it through doing the
internal work
I know the odds I face because how you were wired
I'm just trusting God and his process to receive my
heart's truest desire

8. Look Within

When was the last time you looked within
Questioning why you operate the way you do
Why certain things affect the way you move
Do you think you operate in your highest version of
yourself
These are questions I've proposed to myself after causing
me to lose the love of my life
I slowly had to watch the love we die right in front of my
eyes
Though she was physically there, mentally and
spiritually she had disappeared
I had to seek the Divine for knowledge and true
understanding
It seemed like the Divine sent me all the right info on
front of me to start expanding
Healing my inner child from all his wounds and a new
me started to bloom
I saw the world and it's people in a brand new light
The Divine helped me separate the man from his actions
like mixing water and vinegar

We all have our programming from our parents all the way to society
A lot of it was done on purpose to keep us trapped
Keep us seeking external validation and what's within
You have to get to know the Divine that within all of us, we have to just on in

9. I Appreciate my Spirituality

Where would I be if I didn't have my spirituality
I know I couldn't smile with all the dark clouds that have
been around me
Daily I commit myself to prayer and meditation
Needless to say I've had a life with plenty of bumpy
situations
Yet I still stand strong and not look at those moments to
say they broke me
Rather they were catalysts to allow me to grow and have
a testimony
I've learned my lessons and I cried some tears
My heart has been broken a couple of times throughout
the years
In middle school there was a period I was bullied in
school
One day in P.E. we played basketball with shirts and
skins
Lucky me was chosen for skins
Where at the time I was skinny with small man boobs

Embarrassed by the situation I retreated to myself being
laughed at in school
I even was wrongfully accused of sexual assault at the
end of my military career
Even in that situation I practiced understanding
I even voiced during the investigation I wondered what
demons he had been facing
I never understood why he chose me to lie on
For we never had a bad interaction to look back on
I was confused that he reported on me for this heinous
act
I could say more times I've been in pain but for the sake
of lines I leave it at that
Yet despite it all I still show everyone love
I've never let my pain affect those I've came across
There have been times I've hurt people but not
intentionally
But please know if I did I always try to make it right
eventually
The Divine knows that I haven't been perfect
I lost a few people that were dear to me recently
One of them due to outside influences
I don't know if it was hate or envy
It's just so sad to see that hurt people hurt people
It can even be people who don't even know you
It's just a reflection of them being hurt in their soul
I've always had people who wish the worst for me

I'm sure im not the only who tries to move out of love
can relate to me
I never seek out revenge
The universe balances out what you give
It's a cosmic law of cause and effect
With grace of the Divine I'm always able to push
through
I forgive everyone who has never supported me
I still love everyone despite what has been done against
me

10. If I Could Go Back

If I could go back so many things I would change
I would have sought God sooner to learn how to truly
love
When you're young you experiment with gaining
experience
If I could go back I would have prepared myself better
for you
I would have saved myself for the one I truly loved
Sex is cool but it doesn't feel as good as being a gift
accompanying your heart
All sex does is blind you from behaviors that might split
you apart
Take it from someone who experienced this first hand
There were destructive behaviors I took in my marriage
causing me to lose my best friend
I did the internal work late but only time tell if it was
better than never
It caused me to lose someone I cherished and adored
I'm here to tell to learn from my detrimental mistakes
Do the work and heal from all the pain you have within

Do it for those who you truly love to keep them around
Whether there a lover, family, or a friend
They deserve the best version of you
Wouldn't you want the same offered to you

11. Vibration

Seeing is believing how most people move
People navigate in darkness no matter the time of day
Not realizing that our eyes are limited to one part of the
spectrum
We're not able to see the spirits that interact with us
every day
There's another dimension that our awareness isn't privy
to
We have spirits that surround us wherever you go You're
inaccessible until you change the frequency you're on
The frequency ranges from enlightenment to the lowest
being shame
If you operate from pride, anger, or fear you
unknowingly welcome these evil spirits in
You have to focus on keeping yourself at a high
vibrational state
You have to practice gratitude, act in love, and be at
peace
This is why you have to have self awareness that you
truly love yourself

This is why it's so important to do the work within and
heal pain you've experienced
If you don't then you leave yourself open to evil spirits in
your mind
People don't realize how simple the line hurt people hurt
people
When our needs haven't been met nurtured as needed it
creates a void
Not tending to that creates and molds our personality as
well We tend to hurt people because our perception gets
limited the way we see the world It can be that inner
child ranging from being young to being a teen
We have to do the shadow work to vibrate high
Not doing so will reflect in your relationships
It's all about the law of attraction

12. Apologies to my Soul

I have to apologize to my soul
I cause you so much pain from me not being whole
I took so long to help you heal your wounds
Granted it wasn't something I wasn't aware of doing so
I still know I'm at fault for what I put you through
It took so me long to learn my lessons
You have to know this is why I'm providing this
confession
From here on out you're my top priority
I'll make sure you know that you're loved and will be
kept safe
I'll make sure that anyone I allow my space does the
same
Now that I'm aware that this is my responsibility
I'll make sure that I educate the masses that they have to
take care of their souls as well
We didn't get these lessons as a child or in Sunday
School
It was never in the curriculum to do so
We just were made aware that souls existed

It was never a memo to handle with care
I'm sure if people knew they would take special care of
their individual souls
It would be something parents would teach their
children next to the ABC's
It will definitely be something to teach for the next
generations to come

13. Missing You Dance

I admit in my mind I'm a brand a new me
Yet somehow my heart still moves to same ol beat
That is the tune of wishing to be beside you
Yet I know we don't vibe on the same octaves we used to
For free will is always the instrument of choice
It's on both partners to do the inner work so the night
will remain majestic
Yet unfortunately maybe one partner isn't ready for that
type of forever
Sometimes a partner just isn't ready to dance to that
groove
It's heartbreaking to know that the night was cut so soon
One partner is praying that it's just a pause for just one
song
Then it seems one song becomes two or three, then tears
fall missing the chemistry
We looked so good dancing with one another though at
times we stepped on each other
Either way I missed my dancing partner
Now I'm by myself holding it down on the floor

Always on the lookout wondering if my partner will
come back for more

14. The Wrong One

Coldness is all I feel working itself in
I continue to pray for peace despite the plight
It's my high vibration that the Devil desires for his
appetite
I won't lay down despite the circumstances
Meditation and prayer is my choice of weapons
Positivity is key for me that reigns supreme
The Devil and his minions will have to settle for the
dream
He won't be dining on my pain tonight
For the Divine on my side flips my pain to joy in the
light
He may have won a battle but the Divine will make sure
in the end it's a desirable chapter
Everything that the Devil thought he made me loose
Will come back even stronger than he presumed
For love is a the ultimate secret weapon against folks
with their low vibration stature
All the Devil did is create another beautiful story to
share with those that come after me

The Devil put his bets on the wrong one
He didn't realize that all odds were on one of the chosen
ones

15. New Gig

Everything right now seems like a dream
The life I had no longer seems to be fit for me
For I was booted out like a sitcom with bad ratings
Yet but I'm good, I was the biggest star on that scene
The Divine has me prepping for another job on a set
This next time around should be my biggest gig yet
I just got to get the body right so the light will hit me
just right
No need for a gym it will be just a distraction
I can always workout in the backyard and make it
happen
I'll try no meat this time around to see if my skin will
glow
I hope this time our extras won't be jealous of me being
the co-star in this show
That was the reason I had to leave and hopefully this
show lasts more than a couple of seasons
Oh yeah I was told to run by the studio to pick up the
script
I have to remember that tomorrow I'll set a reminder in

case my mind slips
I'll meditate to keep my mind clear so I'll remain
composed when the cameras appear
The appropriate reaction is paramount when it's time for
the start of the action
I'm grateful to the Divine for me to be still acting

16. From Neo's Point of View

We do live in the matrix
Everything we thought we knew
Is actually a form of manipulation
Everything isn't what it seems
Powers to be created this world of captivity
For we're the actors of this global show
No payment, just our essence being drained so slow
The matrix is acknowledging this world is just a skit
The Devil is in charge using the powers to be as his
puppets
Consequently his puppets are our puppeteers
Who gets paid off our energy to keep us in fear
No judging here, it took me a while to open my eyes
It just sucks when you try to share you get the side-eye
I get a scripture thrown at me instead of them actually
listening
For we could be having free energy
Yet everyone who has gotten a patent has coincidentally
died or came up missing

Do we actually think that was just by chance an accident
Nah that was the Devil getting his two-step in
So I have a scripture as well
For the love of money is the root of all evil
That translates to the motto of this beloved capitalist
country we were born into
Do we think just because our money says In God we
Trust
That we assume it's the Divine not another we speak
about
They poison our foods spiritually and ethically to keep
us sick
If this isn't motivation enough to make you think who
rules this land
I don't mind doing a part two to elaborate more on my
stance

17. No More

No more your touch
No more your voice
No more looking into the windows of your soul
It's all programmed into my memories
No more the present of seeing your lovely face in the
morning
It took forever to get it right but I was still fumbling
hurting you
I wish you knew I was truly all about you
I held on so much because I had a couple of doses of the
essential you
The essential you being healthy with no barriers
between you and I
There were times when we flowed like the currents in
the sea
I always thought you were meant for me
I envisioned us being a beautiful sight to observe
I believed we were supposed to be in heavenly bliss
It was one my top two wishes
The first was being in true enlightenment but with you

by my side
God saw favor with us and we were going to live hella
abundantly on a ride
From our lives, to love, and money
I wanted you to share that beautiful life with
For me, you were my gift
The least I could do was show you direct appreciation for
it

18. Spiritually Awakened

So many people have missed the message
Hopefully through my artistry you can receive the lesson
In the Bible it says we are made in God's image
People truly don't understand what that is truly meaning
For we are the true architect of the world we are living
Through the thoughts we keep we mold the world we
project
Whether it's from our parents, DNA, or our
manufactured society
All these elements combine to mold our thoughts to keep
us in captivity
Rarely do we question the world we've always known
I was one of them until I started questioning how the
system worked
Do realize our mind is powerful as they come
The Divine is seated in all of us
I'm not saying that church doesn't have its place
Just know we don't need a middle man to speak to
Divine when we're already equipped
The true key is being your authentic self being aligned

with your heart and mind
Through actions like sitting in meditation to hear the
Divine's voice
There's no such things as coincidences it's the Divine
speaking through the universe
You must have to do shadow work to totally heal within
We all have beliefs that limit our true potential
Learning to do these things we'll truly to step into our
power

19. Frequency

We all missed the class about frequency and vibration
Or maybe it was elective in high school a subject I just
wasn't into
Nowadays Im all about schooling myself keeping my
vibration high
If you wonder how it's done it's all about staying in a
state of positivity
you have to stay in a frequency of peace and practicing
gratitude
Engaging in activities such as fear or anxiety keeps your
vibration low
That's why if you pay attention to the world it's designed
to keep us divided
They want to keep us in a state of fear so they control
the masses
If you notice that's why everything is set up to divide us
it's one of the oldest tricks of the game that was done
during the times of the Roman Empire
If they keep us divided over race, politics, and religion
People will just keep fighting each other rather than the

system that oppresses them

Jesus and other other ascended masters try to educate us
on how to be light

In the Bible there are some legit teachings but they did
exclude some other crucial info

They didn't make the Gnostic teachings mainstream like
they did the Bible

The Gnostic teachings talks about Jesus teachings that
were geared to go within

If everyone did this we could unite and raise the
vibration

20. Dear Month of August

Dear the month of August
I will never look at you the same
You had to be the hardest time for me to tame
I lost so much that time of the year
I lost a love that resulted in a whole lot of tears
My love's birthday was during that season
Now when it comes around I hide for that reason
I've stayed in solitude desiring to be alone
I rarely want to speak to anyone even on the phone
I was told repeatedly when I was to going to leave
Not knowing the request was only meant temporary but
that's not how it was received
The energy that was given to me made me feel I was no
longer desired on the team
So I left feeling so defeated inside I no longer wanted to
be seen
I knew I made plenty of mistakes that I tried to rectify
I gave my all to prove that she was my ride and die
Yet none of my efforts seem to communicate that to her
no matter what was done

Consequently I had done too much so it seemed I no longer was her one

I don't blame anyone, you're only as good as what the other person thinks should matter

A huge part of me died that day on the scene

I guess that was the reflection of how I made her feel after my emotional infidelity years before I believe

I can't fault her on how she relates and sees me

I paid a huge price to learn how I should have showed up to our marriage

Now that is over I have no desire to find anyone else to start this all over

I pray everyday that I will be forgiven

And hope that she heals and be truly loved as she wishes

I will just fulfill my purpose for the Divine all alone

I'll make it my mission to help others achieve where I failed so they won't lose the one they truly love

21. Grateful to the Divine

I am grateful for where I am
I understand it was all part of the plan
I am grateful for the love the Divine has for me
Without it, I honestly wouldn't know where I would be
I know everything that happens in Divine timing
Everything you receive all is about alignment
I must say I struggled with some type of control
Yet I'm learning it's all about the art of really letting go
What's meant for me will ultimately in the end gravitate
towards me
I must say all my life I naturally allowed my needs to
take a back seat
I recognize that was unhealthy and I should have
allowed others to be there for me
I've learned that is another way I lacked showing my
vulnerability
I'm so appreciative to the Divine to provide clarity so I
may recognize my mistakes
I'm so grateful for the journey that I've embarked on
from going within

Improving myself daily within is elevating my life that I desire externally for me